Norse Mythology

Tales from the Norse Pantheon

Adam Andino

Table of Contents

Introduction: A Brief History of Norse Mythology 1

Chapter 1: The Main Gods 7

Chapter 2: Nordic Creatures and Monsters 18

Chapter 3: Origins of the Norse Pantheon 27

Chapter 4: The Aesir-Vanir War.................................41

Chapter 5: Odin's Sacrifices.....................................51

Chapter 6: Sif and the Golden Hair 57

Chapter 7: Idun and the Golden Apples 62

Chapter 8: The Myth of Fenrir and Tyr 67

Chapter 9: Ragnarok...75

References 83

Introduction: A Brief History of Norse Mythology

While the contrasts of different mythologies could easily be highlighted and debated, the purpose of myths across cultures is the same. What we now call mythology was once religion, and the stories of the religion were used to teach morals, to explain different phenomena, and also to entertain. Religion was, and still is in, today's many societies and frameworks of government, prevalent. Since the beginning of civilization, humans have always been fascinated at the marvels of the world and what could not be explained; hence, the introduction of religions and the wonderings of the afterlife would grip humanity in its many forms. The mythology, or religion, that this book is dedicated to is a particularly fascinating one – Norse Mythology.

The Vikings

The people who believed in the Nordic pantheon were known as the Vikings, originally from the current countries of Norway, Denmark, Iceland, and Sweden. They reigned the seas and land ranging from North America, Greenland, and even as far as Baghdad. Their empire expanded and rivaled even the great Roman Empire. During the Viking Age from 800-1100 CE, they expanded and sought wealth through gold, silver, gemstones, and land.

The Germanic Peoples and Anglo-Saxons

The Germanics were also tossed into the mix as a part of Viking culture. Since the Viking Era encapsulated much of the Northern European regions including the British Isles and the upper regions of the continental Alps, the smaller tribes of the indigenous peoples were often mixed in with Anglo-Saxons and Vikings. While many of their traditions may have mirrored the same principles and ideologies of the Nordic myths, each tribe might have possessed its own unique form of paganism. However, due to the small populations of the tribe and often illiteracy, these myths were lost to time and Christianity.

Oral Traditions

The Vikings spoke in a tongue known as the Old Norse language complete with written runes as the written form. Long before the Vikings wrote down their lore, myths, and legends, they spoke of the stories in the form of oral storytelling and practiced their religion by worshiping the gods in a 'traditional' fashion. There were not a lot of elaborate temples or other places to worship, but instead the gods were worshipped largely in the home, with the stories passed down through generations.

This is not dissimilar to a family's practices in regards to religion, home life, and celebratory days.

Not much is known about Norse mythology itself. There are only a handful of texts that have survived the era. The texts that managed to survive are poems and sagas. The texts *Poetic Edda* and *Prose Edda* were a collection of poems based on the mythologies of the Vikings, along with the sagas, which depicted the lives of Scandinavian kings as well as Germanic heroes such as *Beowulf*. The small collections available were written either in the middle of the Viking Era or right after it during the Dark Ages.

It was also important to note that the religious texts written during the Middle Ages about the Viking Era could have had a Christian influence. Some of the myths and origin stories resemble some of the fables of the Christian mythologies. These texts were written during a time where Christianity was pushing to convert as many as they could into believers, and as such, similar tales to those of the Vikings might have been presented as a conversion tactic.

The Introduction of Christianity

The introduction of Christianity and its dominance took many years to completely eradicate the pre-Christian era of religious mythologies. Before Christianity fought and won the domination of religions, the Christian beliefs in God and Jesus were integrated into the lore of Nordic mythology. This was similar to the Roman pantheon, which also established new deities inspired by Christian stories and merged the deities whose religious views were different. The Vikings often believed in both mythologies.

Christianity eventually led to the downfall of the Viking Era like with so many previously pagan institutions. Around 1000 CE, Christianity became the national religion in Iceland, with the rest of the European countries eventually following suit. Once the Middle Ages were upon Europe, history faded into obscurity until the Renaissance, beginning in the early 15th century.

During the rising annihilation of paganist societies, much of the few Germanic histories and mythologies were destroyed in an attempt to convert the pagans into worshiping Christianity. Many of the pagan practices of the Anglo-Saxons as well as the Vikings were outlawed as Christianity moved to the forefront of unified kingdoms and governments.

Daily Living for the Vikings

The gods, just as in other mythologies, impacted the daily lives of the Germanic and Norse peoples. The perception of the Vikings in modern memory is of seafaring, harsh realities that were the norm. While there is evidence of these Vikings, the lives of most Vikings revolved around agriculture and the home. The sexes were split: women belonged in the home making clothing, cooking and preparing food, and tending to the farm animals such as sheep and cows; men were tasked with plowing the fields, seeding the crops, and crop rotation.

Specialty crafts such as smithing were also available in more populated villages and were often utilized in exchange for food. Famine and raids were rampant throughout the time of the Vikings and affected all. Even the most wealthy and prestigious were affected by diseases and famine.

The Customs of the Vikings

The Vikings did not have an organized religion per se. There were a few places of worship such as temples and halls for the people to gather for celebrations and sacrifices, but they did not resemble the temples as elaborate as, for example, the Greeks and Romans. Instead, they had specific places dedicated to a certain deity such as a grove. There were community-related events such as a sacrifice for war, famine, and even weddings. Humans and animals were often sacrificed when the Vikings believed they had displeased the gods.

The customs implemented with relation to the gods were more personal and familial than one central, rigid religion. While everyone generally believed in the gods and the myths that came with them, it was portrayed throughout historical texts that the Vikings and other Germanic people had personal connections to certain gods and goddesses.

While there are still surviving myths and legends in the Nordic pantheon, there are many holes and convoluted messages within the stories. The historical texts were written for an audience who knew previous information and timelines of the deities and legends. The stories of these deities are also lacking a chronological order, with it not always being clear if Myth A happened before Myth B or vice versa. The lore can be largely confusing and complicated, but the intrigue of the Nordic myths has endured for centuries and is so fascinating that it has inspired myriad books, TV shows, and movies.

In the next chapter, the gods and goddesses of the Norse Pantheon will receive their proper introduction.

Chapter 1: The Main Gods

Odin. Thor. Loki. Thanks to Marvel's *Avengers* saga of comic books and films, the series has given fans a renewed interest in learning more about Norse mythology. Stan Lee, the creator of Marvel Comics, took creative liberties and ideologies from the myths and legends and used them to tell compelling stories about good and evil. Another popular work of fiction that drew inspiration from the Norse Pantheon was *The Lord of the Rings* trilogy by J. R. R. Tolkien, complete with elves, dwarves, and magic. The renewal of superheroes in film and other fictional mediums has resulted in a resurgence of people wanting to learn more about the mythologies of the Nordic people.

Just as with many fictitious retellings, there are massive inconsistencies within the details of the characters in the Marvel universe, such as some characters being inherently good or evil. In the actual myths of Norse Mythology, the realities were not so black and white.

Aesir Deities

There are two subsets of gods in the Nordic pantheon: Aesir and Vanir. Both of the subsets of these deities were powerful and fearful, but they cannot be designated as simply either 'good' or 'evil.' The Aesir deities lived in Asgard, one of the nine realms in the universe, with the lead god Odin. This realm was the location with the most sunshine and the highest branches of a tree known as Yggdrasil. Yggdrasil was the center of all nine cosmos of Nordic mythology, with Asgard as its supreme branch. The tree of life will be covered further in Chapter 3: Origins of the Gods.

Below are the gods in alphabetical order who were associated with this tribe of gods and goddesses.

Baldur: The Peaceful God

Baldur (or Baldr according to some texts and translations) was one of the most peaceful gods in Asgard. He was revered by both gods and men alike for his wisdom, attractiveness, and ability to keep the peace. Baldur was the brother of Thor and the son of Odin and Frigg, the king and queen of the realm. His confidence oozed out of him, leading him to often be the mediator between the humans and the gods to whom they answered. Many scholars often compare him to the Greek and Roman god Apollo, who also was known for his extraordinary beauty and charm.

The eventual death of Baldur led the gods to an event known as Ragnarok, or the end of the era of the gods. It was foretold that Baldur would die due to the involvement of Loki, the trickster god.

Bragi: The God of Poetry

Though not a major god per se, Bragi was the god of poetry and a bard to the court of Odin in Valhalla. In the pre-Christian texts, there was some speculation that Bragi was once a mortal with an affinity for poetry, and those who died and came to Valhalla needed a bard to sing their noble tales and stories. It was also said that the god was the one who welcomed souls from the mortal world to Valhalla. If that was not enough, the god was also believed to be the husband of Idun, the goddess who was responsible for the immortality of the gods.

However, according to some of the recorded texts on Norse mythology during the Middle Ages, it was regarded that Bragi was not a household god, and therefore not worshiped as one in the Norse pantheon. There are many misunderstandings and misconceptions about this particular deity, due to the lack of religious texts surviving from the Viking Era.

Frigg: Queen of the Gods and Goddess of Marriage

Frigg, the queen of the gods and the wife of Odin, ruled over the nine realms. She specialized in marriage, childbearing, prophecy, and wisdom. Although she and Odin had many children together, her most famous child was Baldur, the peacekeeping god. Frigg was second in command after Odin and was the only one aside from him who was allowed to sit on the throne. Often compared to Hera or Juno, the Greek and Roman queens of the gods, she was not the jealous type, but instead had a calm demeanor that was widely respected.

It was believed that the goddess of prophecy had seen the death of her son and the end of the gods long before the events were set in motion.

Heimdall: The Guard of the Realms

Heimdall was the guard of the realms and gates to Asgard due to his incredible strength and eyesight. It was believed that nothing was able to evade him, especially those who tried to break into the realm. He was swift and fearless, traits that also earned him the position of the guardian.

Idun: Goddess of Beauty

Idun was the goddess of fertility, beauty, and youthfulness. She grew the golden apples the gods used for the power of immortality. All the gods wanted to be in her favor so as to possess the youthful glow and energy that would sustain them for thousands of years. She is often compared to the Greek and Roman goddesses Aphrodite and Venus, but not much else is known about her except that she was the wife of Bragi. Much of what is known about her is sadly missing context, and therefore, is a mystery even to this day.

Loki: The Trickster God

One of the most notorious gods in the Nordic myths and legends. Known as the trickster god, he was also the god of fire and a shapeshifter who could change to any creature and gender. Loki was an odd but cunning character, who always acted in self-preservation and for his own amusement. The Marvel films and comics portrayed him as the adopted brother of Thor when in actuality, he was considered to either be a companion or a detriment of the gods.

The god of trickery was often in trouble with the Aesir gods and their enemies alike. He helped to rescue Idun from giants, but then he also killed Baldur, thus causing the beginning of Ragnarok. Loki was the son of an unknown mother and a father who was a giant by the name of Farbauti. Interestingly, Loki was considered neither a household god nor even one worthy of a following. This was perhaps the culmination of all his trickery and open mockery of the Aesir gods.

Loki was portrayed as either god or even possibly giant; not even the texts could agree on what the true form of Loki was.

However, Loki had many offspring with different creatures such as Fenrir, Jormungand, and Sleipner. More about the children of Loki will be discussed in the next chapter where we discuss the creatures and monsters of the Norse myths.

Odin: King of the Gods and the One-Eyed Raven God

Odin, the god of thousands of epithets and names, was the king and ruler of Asgard and the nine realms. Also known as 'the Allfather,' he was the god of poetry, death, war, and even magic. He ruled Asgard with his wife Frigg and had his sons Thor and Baldur. He could easily be compared to Zeus or Jupiter, the Greek and Roman kings of the gods. However, he was much more complex than the adulterous latter gods.

Odin was most notable for sporting an eye patch after sacrificing an eye in the quest for more wisdom. He was a knowledge and wisdom seeker, often going outside Asgard to pursue more knowledge. He was one of the most complex, enigmatic gods in the Nordic pantheon, with traits such as being both a benevolent god and ruthless conqueror with little regard to themes of justice or fairness. He was, much like Loki, only interested in ways to better himself.

The juxtaposition of these traits in this god is one of the reasons why he was revered by all. Not only was he the most powerful deity in the nine realms, his cold demeanor towards justice commanded respect from all. There will be more myths revolving around Odin in the coming chapters.

Thor: The Hammer God

With his trusty hammer Mjolnir, Thor ruled the skies as the lightning and thunder god. He was Odin's most infamous child, more famous than his brother Baldur, because of his superior strength and courage. The Viking warriors often cited Thor as their inspiration for their ruthlessness and bravery in war. Every human warrior aspired to be like him and meet him in Valhalla.

The immense strength that came from Thor was that he was the product of Odin, half-giant, and his mother was a full giant by the name of Jord. Thor was considered to be the protector of the realms, especially Midgard, which is the realm where humans exist. He notoriously had a soft spot for female mortals and often utilized his physique to his advantage.

Thor could easily be compared to the Roman demigod Hercules based on his unmatched strength and physique alone. But that is where the similarities end. Thor also married Sif, his rarely mentioned wife, who had golden hair and became the god of fertility and agriculture. Thor's demise in Ragnarok was also prophesized where he and the Jormungand mutually destroy each other.

Tyr: God of War

The last god of the Aesir pantheon of Norse mythology was Tyr, the Nordic god of war. In contrast to his specialty, the god of war was notoriously fair and just. His moral compass for fairness was unmatched by the other gods. He did not participate in war unless it was the last resort, which was a huge contrast to his counterparts in Mars and Ares, the Roman and Greek gods of war. His character embodied the need for justice, as will be illustrated later in this book where we discuss the myth of Fenrir and Tyr.

Sadly, the lineage of Tyr remains unknown due to the lack of myths and stories related to him. He was a very powerful and important god, but unfortunately, few texts survived which told any substantial information about him.

Vanir Deities

The Vanir deities were those who did not reign in Asgard. The gods and goddesses of this realm were lesser known; not too much was written about the deities. The other aspect that set the Vanir deities apart from the Aesir was that they possessed the knowledge of magic, and therefore, were formidable foes against the Aesir deities during the Aesir-Vanir War, which will be discussed more thoroughly in Chapter 9.

Freyja: Goddess of Magic

Freyja was the daughter of the leader of the Vanir, Njord, and the twin sister of Freyr. She was the goddess of magic, fertility, and lust. The goddess also was believed to be the reason for the introduction of both Aesir and Vanir magic. She was often depicted in her chariot pulled by two cats. Similar to Odin and Valhalla, Freyja was also known to greet half of the fallen soldiers from Midgard to a realm known as Folkvangr, a place with golden fields and peace. The Sessrumnir or 'seat-room' was where they were greeted by the goddess.

Freyja had two daughters by the names of Geresmei and Hnoss with her husband Oor. Together, the four ruled much of agriculture for the humans as they cultivated the mortals themselves.

Freyr: God of Fertility

As Freyja's twin brother and son of Njord, Freyr was the god of fertility, wealth, and tranquility. The god was considered the most benevolent god; sailors often prayed to him for safe passage. He was also the god of male reproduction, as was represented by his myriad of choices of lovers, including goddesses and giantesses alike. One of these goddesses was presumed to be his sister Freyja.

The Vikings often sacrificed boars, his favorite animal, for the celebration of a bountiful harvest or a wedding. Since wealth came in the form of land and crops, the abundance of crops was always followed by expressions of gratitude such as sacrifices to the god.

Njord: The Sea and Wind God

Njord was the leader of the Vanir gods and ruler over the wind and sea. He was also the god of wealth and fertility, as well as sea-faring. His twin children were Freyja and Freyr, also deities of wealth and fertility. However, Njord's specialty and main love was the sea and was even the reason for the split from his wife, the giantess named Skadi, who loved the mountains as her home.

Other than the myth between him and Skadi, Njord remains a relatively unknown god in the scholarly sources of today due to the lack of texts. However, there is a lot of evidence that supported Njord as being a well-known and well-loved god, based on artifacts and evidence of cults on his behalf.

Conclusion

The myths and legends revolving around the gods have remained items of intrigue throughout the centuries. Due to the many holes, inconsistencies, and lack of textual evidence of the pantheon, the deities within the nine realms are enigmatic.

Chapter 2: Nordic Creatures and Monsters

Earlier in this book, it was mentioned how Norse mythology has inspired the great fantasy genre with its crowned jewel being *The Lord of the Rings* trilogy by J. R. R. Tolkien. Many examples of this are the legendary races within the trilogy such as dwarves and elves. While *The Lord of the Rings* might be, perhaps, the most famous example, such a pantheon has inspired the likes of many authors and their fantastical ideas and storylines that are relevant today.

Creatures and Monsters

The creatures and monsters of the Norse pantheon were a collection of races and beings, each from differing realms in the universe. Not all creatures were in opposition to the gods, and sometimes were considered a helping hand within the myths.

Draugr

The draugr were essentially the zombies of the Norse myths, a horde of undead reanimating to cause terror. Some stories indicate that they were similar to modern-day vampires, but the texts describe them more as zombies. Their superhuman strength matched their reek of decaying flesh. The myths claimed the draugr feasted on human flesh and could move through stone walls as if they were phantoms. Their main focus was to guard their treasure troves and to haunt those who had committed atrocities to the draugr while they were still mortals. The draugr could die in two ways: dismembering and burning the body, or if the body itself decayed too much.

Dwarves

The dwarves represented in Norse mythology were not the small men as indicated in popular fantasy books and films. Instead, they lived in the realm of Svartalfheim, or the land of the black elves. This realm was located deep beneath the earth. The dwarves were considered inferior in comparison to men and elves. The greatest asset of the dwarves was their smithing capabilities, with their most famous contribution being Mjolnir, the hammer of the mighty Thor. The dwarves also created many other artifacts within the pantheon, including a boat for Freyr.

Elves

The elves lived in Alfheim, the realm of the god Freyr. They were tall and slender but fit. There were two branches of elves: the light elves known as Ljoslfar, and the dark elves known as Dokkalfar. It is presumed that the dwarves and dark elves were synonymous; they lived under the earth and in the same realm as the dwarves, so they were likely one and the same. The light elves, in contrast, lived in Alfheim with Freyr and were possibly the inspiration for many fictional elves. The light elves were considered to be one of the most beautiful creatures of mythology with golden hair as bright as the sun. They did not interact with humans much unless it was to aid in sickness or to cause disease; basically, it was whatever they felt like doing. Some elves, however, did breed with humans and created half-elf, half-human beings with features of a human with the magical powers of an elf.

Huginn and Muninn

Huginn and Muninn were the two trusted ravens of Odin. 'Huginn' meant 'thought' in Old Norse while 'Muninn' meant 'mind.' The two ravens were the eyes and ears of Odin. Their main task was to fly around Midgard and collect the news of the race of men. With the names meaning 'thought' and 'mind,' it was widely speculated that the ravens were the personification of the expansion of his mind, casting it out to keep track of his subjects. It was also said that one of Odin's greatest fears was that his beloved ravens would not return to him.

Fossegrim

The fossegrim were depicted as water spirits who played the violin in the most beautiful way, and similar to modern-day mermaids, minus the tail. Often the fossegrim were showcased as handsome men with either little or no clothing. They would lead women and children to the water's edge and beyond, causing them to drown. The fossegrim also taught men how to play the violin if they sacrificed a goat in their presence. Depending on the size of the goat, the creature would either teach the men how to play as beautifully as he, or he would teach the men to tune the violin. The thicker and fatter the goat, the more the men learned from the spirit.

Kraken

One of the most infamous creatures of the Norse pantheon, the Kraken often made an appearance with its interference with ships. The Kraken was thought either to be a massive octopus, squid, or even sometimes a crab. Most likely inspired by the giant squids in the deep ocean, the Kraken was said to be the size of an island. When an unsuspecting ship came near to dock and explore the 'island,' it would seize the ship, dragging it and the crew into the depths of the ocean, thus drowning them. It was also recognized that the creature was so massive that its movement created whirlpools, and these would also sink the ships. The Kraken, after killing its prey, then devoured the men who succumbed to drowning.

Norns

The Norns were essentially the Three Fates like in Greek and Roman mythologies. The three Norns decided the fate of each living creature; no one could escape their fate, not even the gods themselves. The three Nords were blind old women who were also the caretakers of Yggdrasil, also known as the Tree of Life. Although they cared for the tree, it was fated to die with Ragnarok. One of the main themes of Norse mythology was that eventually, everything ends and ceases to exist; it is the natural rule of law that cannot be changed.

Ratatoskr

Ratatoskr was a squirrel-like being whose main task was to run up and down the Tree of Life to deliver messages between realms. However, what the creature enjoyed most of all was spreading gossip between the eagle Veorfolnir, who sat atop the Tree of Life, and the serpent Niohoggr, whose lair rested in the roots of the tree. It's alluded that Ratatoskr wanted the two beings to fight against one another and destroy the tree.

Valkyrie

The Valkyrie was perhaps one of the most recognizable creatures in all of the Norse myths and legends. Writers and artists alike have been inspired by the beauty of these mythical creatures. The Valkyries were the helpers of Odin in the battles of men. They were maidens measuring in both beauty and nobility who led the souls slain from battle to Valhalla. However, their name in Old Norse meant 'selector of the fallen.' Not only did these beautiful female spirits ferry the fallen to Valhalla, but they were also the ones who chose who lived and died in battle.

While most of the creatures in this section of the chapter were recognizable, they were somewhat unique to the Norse mythologies with some exceptions. The next section of this chapter describes the children of Loki and the unusual circumstances of their conception and birth.

The Children of Loki

The children of Loki and the creatures he created through shapeshifting deserve their own place in this chapter. Each of the three described below was conceived under strange circumstances: Fenrir, Jormungand, and Sleipner. Each monster and creature were unique in their own right and shattered expectations of the behavior between gods and mortals or other creatures.

Fenrir

Fenrir is perhaps one of the most famous wolves in all of mythology, coming close to the she-wolf in the Romulus and Remus myth of the founding of Rome. Fenrir, however, was not a nurturing she-wolf, but instead the epitome of destruction and nightmarish power. He was the son of Loki and a giantess by the name of Angrboda.

Fenrir made one last appearance in Ragnarok, which will be described in more detail in another chapter.

Jormungand

Jormungand was yet another delightful child of Loki and the giantess Angrboda. This monster took the form of a giant serpent. Jormungand resided in Midgard with a body massive enough to wrap around the entire world. He kept the world in place and constricted with little room to move. In a fit of repulsion, Odin threw him into the ocean where he grew to the size of the earth itself.

The monster was not necessarily nefarious to humans, but he despised the gods. His unbridled hostility towards them, especially toward his arch nemesis Thor, churned within him for thousands of years.

Sleipner

As the last of the children of Loki, Sleipner was a peculiar breed. He was the noble steed of Odin, dark as the blackest of nights and with eight legs. Sleipner was considered to be the greatest horse in all the realms.

The tale of this creature's birth consisted of Loki and the stallion of a giant named Svadilfari. Loki had shapeshifted into a mare or a female horse and was then impregnated by the stallion. After Loki fell pregnant, he carried Sleipner until the creature was born.

Conclusion

The monsters and creatures of Nordic mythology were often both positive and negative influences on gods and mortals. The idea of otherworldly and inexplicable phenomena impacted the way the Vikings expressed their fears and their hopes.

No myth or legend is complete without an origin story. As such, the next chapter will discuss the origin story of the pantheon of the Norse gods.

Chapter 3: Origins of the Norse Pantheon

All stories need a clear beginning, and the Vikings understood this. The Vikings used the origin story of the gods to explain the universe and its creatures. In the times of the Vikings, there was no way of understanding the universe in the same way modern humans do. With this principle in mind, it was necessary to not only explain the origins of men, but to teach lessons of mortality through the same story.

Some aspects of the myth have similarities to other European origin stories such as the Greek origin story involving Zeus. While the stories possess parallels with other ancient myths, other aspects, such as creatures and monsters, are solely unique to the Viking lore.

The Time Before the Gods

Before there were gods, men, and other creatures, there was an emptiness in the universe. This entire universe had three main parts to it: Niflheim, Ginnungagap, and Muspelheim. The three distinct realms of this universe were connected by a singular tree. Each played a part in the existence of the nine realms.

Niflheim

Niflheim was the northernmost tip of the universe with its frigid air and sheets of solid ice. It was a bleak, lifeless place. It could not sustain life, even with its immense water supply frozen in its ice. A stream called Hvergelmir, however, ran through the southernmost tip of the realm; the ice melted into twelve frigid streams. These streams eventually combined to form the rivers of Gjol, which then promptly flowed into the realm of Ginnungagap.

Ginnungagap

Ginnungagap was the realm located in the middle. With a name translating to 'a deep, dark abyss,' there no was no way to sustain life here either in the beginning. The abyss, however, shrunk when the waters of Gjol filled the void in Ginnungagap. The water mixed within the sheets of ice dripped down into Muspelheim, creating the energy and climate to sustain life.

Yggdrasil

With this new thriving climate grew a tree in the middle of Ginnungagap. The tree was known as the Tree of Life, or Yggdrasil. Its roots and branches reached the nine realms and the cosmos that surrounded them, connecting all the realms in one central location. Within the Old Norse runic language, it was said the tree was an ash tree, but scholars have debated that no one knew exactly the species of tree it was.

Muspelheim

Muspelheim was the hottest realm of the cosmos. Also known as the land of fire, Muspelheim was the reason behind the rivers that had begun to flow in Niflheim. As the ice melted, it dripped down to the land of fire, which then sparked and formed mist. The mist and steam swirled around Ginnungagap, resulting in the first living being.

The First Beings

As the sparks caused the steam, mist, and specks of frost to gyrate around Ginnungagap, it started to create a new shape. Within this shape was the first frost giant, or Jotunn, called Ymir, the first living being.

Ymir

After the creation of Ymir, he slumbered for eons; as he slept, the sweat from his armpits and the meat from his legs formed into three other Jotunn. Their hearts were plagued by cruelty and wickedness, and therefore, were the eventual enemies of the gods.

The Primordial Cow and the Gods

After Ymir and his children were constructed into existence, a tremendous cow by the name of Audhumla was also formed. She licked on the ice as she suckled Ymir and his family of giants. She grew tired of the taste of nothingness from the ice and snow. As she licked, she found solid rock underneath it. Enticed, she continued to lick the ice until two days later another shape started to form. The face of another being was visible.

On the morning of the third day, Audhumla licked the form of the first godlike being into existence. He was attractive, good-natured, and powerful. He was named Buri, and as he glimpsed his new world and onto the giants, he recognized their evil nature.

Buri eventually became the father of two children, a son called Borr and a daughter called Bestla. In some translations and versions, Bestla was considered to be the daughter of Ymir, born out of the armpit sweat of her father. Therefore, all gods had the presence of giants within them as they furthered their lines.

Giants Versus Gods

Borr and Bestla married and had three sons together known as Vili, Ve, and Odin. They watched as the giants ruled over the realms with a mighty fist and cruelty at every turn. In a revolution, the three sons of Buri and Bestla slayed the Frost Giants after enduring many years under the cruel giants' rule.

Forming the Nine Realms

Ymir was the first to fall out of the Jotunn. As he lay dead in the middle of the Ginnungagap, his body overtook the entirety of the realms. His blood gushed from his wounds, creating massive torrential rivers, which drowned the rest of the frost giants, save for a few, who were able to continue the line of the giants, otherwise known as the Jotnar, by the Norse people.

Mountains Out of Bones

After Ymir fell dead in the center of the universe, his body encompassed the entire cosmos. It was decided by Odin and his brothers to use the body as the foundation of the new world. From this point, the brothers dismantled the body of the once-fearsome giant.

Every part of the body of the frost giant was used. The brothers dragged the bones and crafted mountains and valleys, as they did not want the new worlds to be flat and dull. The blood of the giant was transformed into the bodies of water such as oceans, lakes, seas, rivers, and springs. Fragments of teeth and bone were ground into fine dust, contributing to the sand and rocks of the land of Midgard.

The brains of the mountainous creature were fashioned into clouds; his hair became all plant life such as trees, flowers, and grass on both land and sea. The top of the skull of the mighty Ymir was crafted into the archway of the heavens. His flesh became the dirt as it covered the ground of the world.

The Final Formations of Midgard

With the world almost finished, the brothers realized something was missing in the sky. One of the brothers suggested using sparks from the fires burning below in

Muspelheim. The gods released millions of sparks from the depths to create a speckled sky at night. Each tiny glimmer represented a duty and held a name attached to it as it rotated across the sky every night. The deities reasoned it would be a way for the mortals to navigate their way back home from their wanderings.

The last touch was the eyebrows of the giant. To prevent the giants from entering the world of the planned mortals, the eyebrows were crafted into a protective barrier to keep them away.

Upon completion, the new world for mortals was called Midgard, as it was placed in the middle of Ginnungagap and Yggdrasil. The new world would be in the prime location from which the deities were able to watch over them. Jotenheim, the realm of the giants, surrounded the new world.

The First Mortals

Humans were not the original inhabitants of Midgard. With the remaining rotting flesh of Ymir, the three brothers crafted the first beings of the realm, which were the dwarves. They enjoyed living in the deep underground of the earth and crafting things. The gods, realizing their mistake, moved the dwarves to their eventual home in Svartalfheim.

With the second and final trial, the gods wove two figures out of two trees, which then created the first man and woman, Ask and Embla. Ask was carved out of an ash tree, and therefore given his name, while Embla was carved from an elm tree. The gods breathed life into the mortals and bestowed upon them the gifts of wisdom, speech, sight, sound, and intelligence.

Vili and Ve were absent after the creation myth; as for their whereabouts and what happened after the creation of the nine realms, those stories have been lost to time.

The Nine Realms

The gods built the Nine Realms presumably around the same time as they built Midgard. With all the chaos and destruction, it was necessary to rebuild a new home they could inhabit until the end of their reign, or Ragnarok. As they built the layers of the cosmos, they decided to place their realm at the top. This would ensure their creations would be protected from the frost giants. Their solution was to create a rainbow bridge, or Bifrost, as the main transportation portal to other realms if needed.

The realms included Asgard, Alfheim, Hel, Jotunheim, Midgard, Muspelheim, Svartalfheim, Nifelheim, and Vanaheim.

Asgard

Asgard was known as the realm and home of the Aesir gods, and therefore, is considered to be a peaceful landscape compared to the mortal world. It was portrayed as a divine city with tall towers made of the most immaculate silver and gold and a wall to keep out unwanted visitors. The Bifrost was connected to Midgard and the other realms to ensure safe passage for the gods to do their bidding.

Odin became the main overseer and was known as the 'Allfather' for both gods and mortals. The great hall known as Valhalla was the location where Odin himself greeted the mortals who honorably died in battle.

Alfheim

Alfheim was located in the heavens not too far away from Asgard. It was the home of the light elves and of the Vasir god Freyr, who reigned there. Magic ran rampant in Alfheim, which was composed of mystical beings and vegetation. The light elves were responsible for giving mortals the creativity to create art, music, and other forms of self-expression.

Hel

Otherwise known as Helheim, Hel was a gloomy hellscape located beneath the roots of the Yggdrasil. It was originally constructed with walls and only one gate to enter and exit. There was only one paved way to Hel called Helveg, and it wound down the roots of the tree until the entrance to the gate. Hel was ruled by the aptly named goddess known as Hel, the daughter of Loki and sister of Fenrir and the serpent of Midgard.

Eventually, Hel was populated with the souls of the dead who passed because of old age or disease. It was believed that, similar to Greek and Roman mythologies, there were several layers of the underworld, including Valhalla; however, it is uncertain how the souls lived out the remainder of eternity or how many levels there were.

Jotunheim

Jotunheim, otherwise known as Utgard, was the realm that surrounded Midgard and was home to the Frost Giants. It was considered the birthplace of magic and wilderness in its most chaotic form. It was also where the god of trickery Loki originated. Jotunheim was connected to Asgard by a river called

Iving, a treacherous river to cross with swelling rapids and frozen blocks of ice.

Midgard

Midgard was the realm of humans. After this realm was created by Odin and his brothers, they placed massive barriers around the land to protect the helpless mortals from Frost Giants and other malicious beings. The gods also created all the animals and creatures within the realm.

Muspelheim

Muspelheim was an essential piece in the creation of the universe and all the creatures within it. Muspelheim was home to the creatures known as the Muspells or the Fire Giants. Their leader or father, scholars did not know which, Surtr, ruled over the realm. It was believed that Surtr, along with the other Muspells, had only one reason for existence, as they only ever were presented one time in the ancient texts. Their role was to eventually rise from the depths of Muspelheim once Ragnarok began.

Svartalfheim

The dwarves, also known as the dark elves, ruled over the realm of Svartalfheim, otherwise referred to as Nidavellir. The realm was deep within the earth; the only lights were dimly lit torches and the forges of the dwarves. The dwarves thrived in this environment. Without the distractions that could be found in other realms, it was easy for the dwarves to focus and hone in on their craftsmanship. They created many weapons of the gods, such as Mjolnir, and even built boats for the god Freyr. With both superior craftsmanship and the ability to weave magic into their work, the dwarves were, by far, the most elite weapon makers of all nine realms.

Nifelheim

Both Nifelheim and Muspelheim were among the oldest realms in the universe. While both of the realms were directly responsible for the creation of all life, Nifelheim was the only realm without inhabitants. It was an icy, frozen wasteland with mist swirling around its top. It was believed, at first, that the dead walked in Nifelheim. However, after Odin threw the goddess Hel into her own realm, the dead souls wandered around the depths of Hel instead. From that point, Nifelheim remained quiet and still.

Vanaheim

The last of the nine realms was called Vanaheim, and was home to the Vanir gods. It was assumed that the realm itself was full of magic, light, and the home of various mystical plants and animals. The Vanir deities specialized in fertility and agriculture. The magic and gifts of the gods translated to lush, beautiful gardens and crops. With abundant harvests, sunshine, rain, and low-powered winds, Vanaheim was the paradise of realms other than Asgard. The oceans and seas within the realm often had favorable weather conditions for those who loved to journey on the seas and fish in the depths. It was one of the most pleasant, relaxing realms of the universe.

It was widely believed that the laxness of the realm caused a major issue with the gods in Asgard, thus resulting in the Aesir-Vanir War. More of the story and the consequences of the war will be discussed in the next chapter.

Conclusion

Back before humans understood the universe and the depths of its expansion, Norse mythology explained how the cosmos burst into existence. Their understanding, or lack thereof, of the universe was extremely limited. As was in human nature, the questions of how the world began were asked and answered. Similar to other mythologies in Greece and Rome, it was the king of all the deities who constructed the world and created mortal, living humans.

In Norse mythology, the king of the deities Odin and his two brothers crafted the realms from the bones of their greatest fallen enemy: a literal landscape for the rebirth of a new era. The nine realms of the world coexisted with each other; often the gods visited the home of their newest and most beloved creation, the humans. Midgard was placed in the middle of the realms, which indicated the importance of mortals.

Even though the realms coexisted together, it was not always harmonious. The Frost Giants and other sinister beings constantly threatened gods and mortals alike. A lot of times, however, the threats came from the deities themselves.

Chapter 4: The Aesir-Vanir War

The Aesir-Vanir War happened after the nine realms were created. The war was, according to the texts, the first war since the inception of the realms. The Aesir—those living in Asgard— and the Vanir—those who lived in Vanaheim—waged a long, bloody, and intense war between themselves. This in-fighting amongst the gods was felt throughout the entirety of the realms, causing uprisings and fear among the people.

Reasons Behind the War

While it was not fully clear the causation of the war, its effects lasted until Ragnarok. Gods and goddesses on both sides were forced out of their homes to move into the opposite realm as a peace token. Some scholars believe that it was a culmination of the differences of values, the ever-growing popularity of the Vanir deities amongst humans, and the incest that was prevalent throughout Vanaheim that led to the war. One story, however, remains the most popular theory of instigation.

Intense Jealousy

After the creation of mortals, both Aesir and Vanir gods demanded loyalty and sacrifices to be made in their name. The Aesir were, at first, the more respected of the two races of gods. They held more power over humans, and therefore, had more claim to the mortals.

Over time, it was believed that the perspective of the humans shifted. While the Aesir gods still were given more sacrifices, they began to notice the popularity of the Vanir deities over themselves. The deities of Vanaheim wanted an equitable share of the glory and the respect of the humans.

This jealousy could have gotten out of hand between the gods. The Vanir gods represented the bountiful fertility of both agriculture and bearing children. The two direct needs of food and reproduction were the specialty of the Vanir, and therefore commanded more respect and love from the mortals who worshiped them.

Incestuous Relations

While the intense jealousy may have been a contributing factor, it was not the only reason for the war. The Vanir deities were known for incestuous relations with each other. Njord and his sister, who remained unnamed, were the supposed father and mother of twins Freyja and Freyr. It was also believed that the twins had multiple lovers, including each other.

The Aesir gods did not agree with this lifestyle and therefore grew disgusted with the thought of incest in Vanaheim. The compounding factors of incest, jealousy, and the introduction of shamanistic magic in Asgard were enough for the gods to wage war with each other.

The Magic of Gullveig

The magic Gullveig possessed was the darkest magic known in the realms, called seidr. It was considered to be shamanic magic and often led to destruction. The magic swayed the fates of mortals and gods alike and often ended with the death of someone.

Gullveig

In some translations and beliefs, Gullveig was the goddess Freyja who entered Asgard. The beautiful goddess taught her magic to the many deities who were interested in her magic and ability to bend one's fate.

After a while, the magic was abused. The values of the deities were in jeopardy. Self-absorption interfered with the values of truth, honor, justice, and loyalty. After realizing they had cast their core values off to the side in the pursuit of selfish desires, they held Gullveig accountable instead of themselves.

Thrice-Killed Gullveig

In response to the introduction of such dark magic, the Aesir gods tortured and killed the goddess three times. They repeatedly stabbed her with spears until her first death and burned her body twice. Each time she was killed, her body emerged from the ashes of her previous life. The power the goddess possessed struck hatred and fear into the hearts of the Aesir gods, rivaling the power of even Odin himself.

The Aesir deities believed Gullveig to be either a master of sabotage or a spy for the Vanir. Combined with her power of resurrection each time she was murdered, the fear escalated into hatred for her and the rest of the Vanir deities.

On the other side of the spectrum, the Vanir were enraged at the thought the Aesir gods had purposefully attempted to murder one of their own. In an outrage, they prepared themselves for war. The righteous justice and vengeance they felt prompted them to clamor against the gates of Asgard for war.

The First War Between Gods

The first scene of the war branded Odin as the defender of the realm. The start of the war was caused by the spear Odin threw into the Vanir army, killing one of the gods. Enraged, the spark of battle blazed into a fiery war.

Over a long period of time, both sides engaged in a war for dominance. The war was intense and bloody. The Aesir, known for their brute strength, used weapons and hand-to-hand combat in the battles against their foes. The Vanir cast magic spells and used them to their advantage.

Murky Winners

As the war continued to wage, it was clear that no side could overthrow the other. The gods on both sides were evenly matched. No force was better than the other. The tides of war consistently changed direction to favor both tribes of deities, leading to a stalemate.

After a long period, both sides grew weary of the struggles between them. It was clear there was no winner, only a bloodbath between the two tribes of divinity.

A Truce and a Hostage Negotiation

In Viking culture, it was customary that two warring villages or peoples ended a war with a truce and a negotiation of hostages. It was seen as a good faith ritual that the villages would continue to live in peace.

The Truce

After both sides agreed to end the war, there was much negotiation between the Vanir and Aesir gods. The sides bickered about the reason for the start of the war. According to the Vanir deities, it was the fault of the Aesir, and therefore, they should pay retribution by sharing in the number of sacrifices and favors.

Eventually, both sides decided to live as equals in peace. The discussion was a long-drawn-out conversation between the gods to decide the best course of action. In addition to the truce, there was to be a hostage exchange between the rival tribes.

The Hostage Exchange

After the tribes committed to the truce, the next step was to arrange for the hostages. From the Aesir deities were two brothers of Odin: Hoenir, a swift-legged but slow-tongued god of silence, and Mimir, a god of wisdom. The Vanir produced the twins Freyr and Freyja alongside their father Njord, the ruler of the Vanir.

The five gods departed to their new homes. The three previous Vanir gods settled into their new homes with ease. Freyr and Njord became overseers of the sacrifices the humans made, while Freyja taught the Aesir gods of magic used in Vanaheim. Unfortunately, the previous Aesir gods did not do so well in the adjustment.

A Beheading, Then a Cauldron

Hoenir and Mimir originally adjusted well. The Vanir, noticing the strength and beauty of the god Hoenir, appointed Hoenir as the new ruler. The adjustment at first fit both Vanaheim and the gods well; Hoenir appeared to have a grasp of the concept of ruling with Mimir by his side.

We Were Cheated!

However, the presence of Mimir and the inability of Hoenir to make decisions without the aid of Mimir were detrimental to the arrangement. Strength and attractiveness were not enough to make a leader out of a slow god. Hoenir was also an inadequate ambassador. He spoke without a clue and believed in letting others decide on the solution instead of him assuming responsibility.

The Vanir believed they had been cheated in assets. Not only was Hoenir a sham, but they also suspected that Mimir did not possess the wisdom that was originally conveyed. In retaliation to the Aesir gods, they beheaded Mimir and sent the head back to Odin as both a challenge and a threat.

Odin maintained his composure. The beheading of his brother had upset him. To prevent another war, Odin instead enchanted magic spells and poetry over the severed head and wrapped it in herbs. He then placed the preserved remaining part of his brother into a spring at the base of the Yggdrasil tree, known as Mimir's Well. Odin visited the spring often in search of wisdom, especially in times of great need.

Spit in the Cauldron, Please

Exhausted from the drama and constant fighting between the Aesir and the Vanir, the gods convened to rectify another truce. It was decided that it was a massive misunderstanding; the fighting needed to end. Both sides agreed on this sentiment. Instead of opting for violence, one of the gods grabbed a cauldron and instructed each god from Asgard and Vanaheim to spit in it.

As the saliva from all the gods mixed, it formed the wisest being in the cosmos known as Kvasir. Upon entering the world, he became a traveler among the realms and distributed wisdom to all he met. Nevertheless, the existence of Kvasir was the true end of the Aesir-Vanir War and the beginning of the gods living among each other in peace.

Conclusion

The Aesir-Vanir War was the first war that was waged after the inception of the nine realms. It was a long, bloody, and intense war that ended in the beheading of a god of wisdom and the birth of a new one.

Many scholars believed that the war was a depiction by both the Scandinavian and Germanic people. The Scandinavian pantheon included mainly the Aesir gods, while the pantheon of the Germanic people was constructed with the Vanir gods. The war was a metaphor for the two peoples to finally come together in peace after many years of war in evenly-matched battles.

Chapter 5: Odin's Sacrifices

The common sacrifice for one to obtain knowledge and wisdom is time, and in modern-day societies, money. To be considered a master of a skillset, it is typically required to invest 10,000 hours into learning and building upon what is already known. Money, especially in the pursuit of degrees and certifications, is also necessary in today's society.

But what about sacrificing a part of the body; an eye, for example? How about subjecting oneself to death to pursue the knowledge they sought?

Odin and His Quest for Knowledge

As the ruler of Asgard and overseer of the nine realms, it was crucial that Odin acquire knowledge in any given circumstance. He longed for the infinite wisdom and truth of the realms. Odin constantly was on the quest for this wisdom. He wanted to learn the intricacies of magic, prophecy, and the inner workings of the universe.

Odin wanted to learn and understand everything. The price for such knowledge, however, was one he often paid heavily.

Odin and the Sacrificial Eye

Odin, in comparison to the rest of the gods, was superior in wisdom and intellect. He was, after all, one of the first gods to roam and eventually overthrow the original Frost Giants before the birth of the nine realms. The powers of Odin, however, were limited based on what he knew. To expand his intellect, he decided to pursue the knowledge of his decapitated brother Mimir.

Odin, the One-Eyed God

Mimir was placed in a fresh, trickling spring under the roots of the tree Yggdrasil, where the waters teemed with secrets and truths of the universe. Mimir drank from the spring every day, and therefore, he was gifted with all the wisdom any deity could possess. Often, Odin came to his brother in times of great need of the wisdom Mimir had to offer; other times, it was purely to coerce him into sharing the knowledge with him. Mimir was superior to Odin in wisdom; in his mind, Odin needed to surpass the level of intellect his brother had.

Mimir knew how much Odin wanted to have the infinite wisdom of the universe. Mimir warned Odin that such a request would have a steep price to pay. In order to grant Odin access to a drink of the crisp, clear liquid, Odin had to give up something in return.

Odin thought for a moment of something worthy of the depth of knowledge. In a fluid motion, he gouged out one of his eyes and flicked it into the spring. With the sacrifice received, Odin was allowed to drink from the Mimisbrunnr, otherwise known as the Well of Knowledge. From that moment forward, he was considered to be the most mentally and intellectually powerful of all the gods. No one could ever outmatch him.

Confusion Over Which Eye

While the texts do not say which eye he gave up, it was quite clear that to proceed with becoming the wisest of all the gods, intense sacrifice was a necessity. Artists over the millennia have developed their unique perspectives on which side the god removed his eye. In some illustrations, he was shown with his left eye missing; in others, it was his right.

Odin and the Hanging from the Yggdrasil Tree

One of the other myths revolving around Odin and his sacrifices was his hanging from the Yggdrasil tree in his pursuit of knowledge. The myth illustrates his inherent need to pursue further knowledge and what he would do to obtain that knowledge. Previously, he surrendered his eye for enlightenment. What else would he be willing to give?

The Norns

After the goddess Freyja introduced magic to the realm of Asgard, Odin noticed she was able to read runes to change the fate of a person. Curious, he then went to find the Norns who also dictated the fates of gods and mortals alike. As he observed their magic under the Yggdrasil tree, he discovered they also used runes to deliver the final fates to the mortals.

In his jealousy and hunger for more knowledge, he asked the Norns what was necessary to gain the same knowledge they had; they responded he must hang upside-down on the Yggdrasil for a number of days and nights without aid.

Up Goes the God

Odin agreed to their challenge. He hung upside-down from the Yggdrasil tree for nine days and nights: one for each realm. With a flair for the dramatic and to prove how committed he was to gain the knowledge of the runes, he stabbed himself with his spear.

The Aesir gods were to abstain from helping him. During those nine days and nights, he starved himself. He refused to eat or drink anything. Eventually, his body shut down and he died while hanging from the tree. Dried blood pooled around him while his body shriveled from a strong, powerful god to a hollow, gaunt one.

After his death on the ninth night, he was then resurrected, renewed, and with the knowledge of the magical runes. He was now the singular most powerful being in the cosmos. With this new knowledge, he learned nine magical songs and 18 extremely powerful enchantments. Not only could he heal physical and emotional wounds, but the weapons of his enemies were now rendered useless as he learned how to constrict their movements.

Conclusion

The myths of the sacrifices of Odin revolve around a central theme to remind the recipient of the story there were sacrifices necessary in the pursuit of knowledge. The devotion to knowledge often meant that he was willing to give up a part of himself to learn more, and therefore become more powerful. The story resonates even today. While the sacrifices needed to learn things don't need to be as extreme as Odin's, it is a reminder that anything worth knowing will require some sort of sacrifice.

Chapter 6: Sif and the Golden Hair

The story of Sif, wife of Thor, is one of the few legends surrounding the goddess of the harvest. Her long, golden hair was her most prized trait. Loki, the god of trickery, had a devilish plan up his sleeve to play a prank on the beautiful but vain goddess. The story deals with despair, a threat, and a promise kept.

Sif and Her Hair

The goddess of the harvest, Sif, had the most beautiful golden hair of all the realms. Rivaling the beauty of even Freyja herself, Sif was the wife of Thor. She loved him deeply and even bore him children. Sif was the pride and joy of the god of thunder, especially with her long, luscious golden locks.

Sif was an important goddess to the Vikings. Her hair represented the golden wheat fields, but she was also associated with passion, the sun, fertility, and agriculture.

Loki and His Prank

Loki, the god of trickery, wanted to prank Thor and his family.

While Sif slept, he chopped off her beautiful golden locks. Only stubble remained. Satisfied with his work, he vanished into the night. However, upon waking, Sif immediately noticed her head felt unusually light. She ran her fingers through the stubble, realizing that she had no hair left. Her husband awoke to her sobbing. Immediately, he went to find Loki, whom he knew was behind the horrible prank.

Loki knew that Thor would come looking for him. He shapeshifted into various forms to fool the god, but eventually, Thor caught hold of him. He threatened Loki; if the god did not rectify his mistake, Thor would crush every bone in his body. Loki knew the god did not make those threats lightly, and therefore, went off on a quest to find a wig for the mortified Sif.

Loki and the Dwarf Brothers

Loki ventured to the realm of the dwarves known as Svartalfheim. The dwarves generally did not interfere with the gods unless there was a job that needed to be done; in this case, Loki promised the favor of the Aesir gods and himself. He entered the cave of Ivaldi, home to two dwarven brothers named Brokk and Eitri.

Brokk and Eitri

Loki charmed the brothers by praising their superior skills compared to the rest of the dwarves. When Loki requested that they make Sif a golden wig fused with magic, the brothers began their work. The god neglected to tell them the reason behind the wig. Loki did, however, offer them the eternal gratitude of both Sif and Thor, as well as a favor from him and the rest of the gods.

As the brothers worked, he pulled Eitri aside and quietly praised him for his superior smithing to that of his brother. Privately pleased, he agreed to work on another project for Loki. However, Brokk overheard them speaking and secretly started another project of his own in a competition with his brother.

The Golden Wig

The wig was finished. The pure gold of the wig had fine strands that were close to the form of hair. The locks were embedded with magic so that the wig would then regenerate the original hair of the goddess swiftly. Both dwarves were pleased with the project, and Loki himself expressed his gratitude.

Gungnir

Eitri presented his project first. It was a spear finely crafted and perfectly balanced. Not only was it superbly crafted, but it was also magically imbued with the power to never miss its target. Loki knew that this would please Odin, for he feared the anger of the Allfather. He graciously accepted the gift from Eitri and awaited the project of Brokk.

Skidbladnir

Brokk presented a massive ship for the god, called Skidbladnir. The ship could hold all the gods in Asgard judging by its immense size, but there was magic at play as well. Skidbladnir also had favorable winds in its sails and was easily folded until it could fit into a pocket. Loki was impressed by the craftsmanship Brokk had provided. The god knew it would make a stupendous gift for Freyr, who would greatly appreciate this.

The Return of Loki

Loki left the dwarven realm and made his way to Asgard. Upon his return, Thor questioned if the trip had been successful. Loki beamed with pride and presented the wig to Sif. Its bright golden presence illuminated the face of the goddess, who fell instantly in love with the remedy to her problem.

She placed the wig on her head, and soon her original hair started to grow back to its former glory. Upon glimpsing the hair that flowed from his wife's head, he exclaimed that her golden hair was more beautiful than it had ever been. With this validation, Sif was no longer upset. It seemed that all was forgiven for the time being; Thor and Sif left Loki to present the two other gifts to Odin and Freyr, who both equally enjoyed them.

Conclusion

The Vikings used the myth as an explanation for the wheat to be shorn when it was ready to harvest. The story was another reminder to the Nordic peoples to remain hopeful after trials and tribulations. After all, the beauty of life was that, even though some surprises may be unwelcome, they can be turned into something of greater value.

Chapter 7: Idun and the Golden Apples

Idun, the goddess of beauty, held the key to immortality in her garden rich with various fruits and flowers. The most valuable product of her garden, however, was her golden apples. The golden apples were the sustenance of the gods. Similar to the Greek mythology of ambrosia, which was the sustenance of their pantheon, the apples were fresh and contained the magic of immortality within them.

Idun was the wife of Bragi, the god of poetry, and the daughter of the dwarf blacksmith known as Ivald. After she married Bragi, she ascended to the realm of Asgard, and with her, the chest of the golden apples she carried. Her chest always remained full, even after the gods had almost emptied it daily.

The Danger of Power

Because she possessed the fruit, she was often the target of dwarves and giants alike who wanted to become immortal. She kept careful watch on her prize; one small mistake would prove to be detrimental to her and the gods.

To Trust the God of Trickery

Loki, Odin, and Hoenir were on another quest when, as they were about to head home, they stopped and killed an ox. They proceeded to cook it, but the meat refused to cook. An eagle called down from the branches of the top of a nearby tree, pleading for the gods to feed it or it would not allow the meat to cook. The gods begrudgingly agreed, and the eagle picked out the best cuts of meat and flew away.

In a fit of rage, Loki shapeshifted into a hawk and chased the eagle. Unfortunately, the eagle was the giant Thjazi. The giant held Loki in his clutches, refusing to release him. He threatened Loki that he would return and kidnap him if he didn't bring the apples of Idun directly to him. Loki agreed, and he was released by Thjazi.

After the three gods returned from their quest, Loki immediately set off to find Idun and her chest of apples. He lied and told her that, on his travels, he found apples that were just as magnificent as the ones she possessed. She should bring them and compare the two types of fruit. Convinced by the silver tongue of the god, she followed him until they reached the walls beyond Asgard and entered into a forested area.

The Kidnapping of Idun and the Golden Apples

After she reached the edge of the forest near the bottom of a mountain range, Thjazi grabbed the goddess and her apples. He brought her to the heart of Jotunheim, the realm of the giants, and into his home. The home of the giant was situated on the top of the highest mountain peak. The wind howled as ice decorated the inside of the abode. The giant had the goddess in his clutches.

After Idun left Asgard, the gods began to feel their ages. Wrinkles appeared on their faces, and they began to physically feel weak. Their hair grayed. The gods of Asgard searched for her but could not find her. One of the gods reported that they had last seen the goddess with Loki. Once they caught him, he confessed what had happened to his fellow deities. He was then given a mission: if he did not retrieve the goddess and her apples, he would be killed as punishment for his crimes.

The Retrieval of the Beloved Goddess and the Apples

Loki made haste to rescue the goddess from the giant. He once again shapeshifted into a hawk and flew across the barrier of Asgard into Jotunheim. Once the god crossed the threshold of Jotunheim, he scoured the mountain peaks and discovered the goddess was alone in the palace of the giant, who had gone to the ocean to fish. Loki quickly turned her into a nut and carried her, along with the golden apples, in his talons.

Once the giant returned from his fishing trip, he realized the goddess was gone. He saw a hawk in the distance and knew exactly what had happened. He then turned back into his eagle state and pursued the hawk. The giant easily closed the gap between himself and Loki, whose wings flapped furiously.

There Was Smoke and Fire!

The Aesir gods waited for Loki's return. In the distance, they saw the god of trickery being followed by a massive eagle. They devised a plan to fortify the entrance to Asgard with fire as soon as Loki crossed the border. Kindling the border, they readied themselves to light it.

The giant Thjazi was dangerously close to Loki. One swoop of the mighty talons of the eagle and the mission would have failed. Loki zoomed past the border and the gods immediately struck the kindling to create a burning wall on the border.

Thjazi was moving too quickly to stop before he hit the flames. He could not stop or transform into his giant form; instead, he flew straight into the blazing border and burned to death. Idun and her apples were restored to their rightful place in Asgard.

Conclusion

The lesson to be extracted from the myth was to be wary of those with a silver tongue; they may not always have the best intentions. Loki was notorious for his trickery, and that was what led to the kidnapping of Idun. Her blind trust in the god of trickery and the lack of faith in herself and her gift proved to be troublesome for her. If Loki was not forced to rescue her by the Asgardians, her fate would have been a different tale. The myth was a cautionary tale. The myth was also used to illustrate the importance of Idun as a goddess.

Chapter 8: The Myth of Fenrir and Tyr

There are many myths surrounding the children of Loki: the goddess Hel, who was the daughter of the god; Jormungand, one of his sons who circled the world in an eternal rivalry with Thor; and Fenrir, the eldest son of the god.

Fenrir, as mentioned previously, was a massive wolf who was destined for destruction. He played a major role during Ragnarok, which will be discussed in the next chapter.

Fenrir as a Young Pup

The fate of Fenrir was known by the gods alone. Because they knew what destruction and chaos he was capable of, it was deemed that Fenrir was to stay in Asgard with the gods to keep an eye on the young beast. Not much was known about the creature after he was born; it was entirely possible that because the gods knew of his fate, he was subjected to abuse and other misgivings.

The Chains That Bind Me

The only god to even approach the wolf was Tyr, the god of war. Tyr, despite being the god of war, was surprisingly calm, collected, but most importantly, fair. The god fed and reared the wolf, who grew up very quickly.

The gods, noticing the new size and strength of the wolf with each passing day, decreed that the wolf be chained to a tree. Their fear overpowered any reason; fear of the wolf and the prophecy of the destruction caused by the wolf was stronger than anything else. Odin listened to their demands and reassured the gods that Fenrir would be bound.

Fool Me Once

The first attempt to bind the wolf to a tree was not successful. The gods tricked the wolf into thinking his bindings were a test of strength. Eager to please his masters, he broke through the chain with one swift kick. To prevent anger and possible bloodshed from the wolf, the gods clapped and cheered at the success.

Fool Me Twice

The gods repeated the process, except this time with a thicker, heavier chain. Fenrir agreed to be bound to a tree with this chain. He attempted to break free, but could not at first. He wanted to check the strength of the binding before utilizing his full power, which then snapped it in half. For the second time, the gods applauded and cheered at the newfound success, but something was off. The audience cast side glances at one another while others frowned.

Fenrir began to put the pieces together of the bindings and the want to test his power. The cheers sounded instead hollow and afraid; it did not take him long to figure out they were afraid of him, although he did not know why.

Gleipnir: The Unbreakable Chain

Now nervous, the gods sent a message to the dwarves. It was of the utmost importance to craft the strongest chain they could. Magic, the Asgardians decided, was the only thing that could truly hold him. The dwarves faced the challenge and produced a chain that was extremely light and thin compared to the previous two chains. The magic was fashioned by the impossible: the sound of footsteps of a cat; the breath of an oceanic fish; the roots of a mountain; the beard of a beautiful and fair maiden; and the saliva of a bird. The chain was called Gleipnir.

Never Trust an Asgardian

After the chain was finished, they attempted to trick Fenrir a third time. Fenrir had a nagging suspicion that the gods were up to something. This enraged the massive wolf, who had grown exponentially since the last time they tried to chain him. He kept his suspicions at bay until the third chain was brandished.

The wolf called to Odin, with his suspicions high. It was no secret that he and Odin never got along. Odin had never been present before, so why was he here now? Odin tried to calm the beast by telling him it was a joke and not to fear him. Fenrir, however, sniffed out the lies on his breath.

Fenrir immediately recognized the work of the dwarves from the size of the chain itself. He recalled the size of the previous chains; this one was much lighter. Magic must have been used, and the only race clever enough to imbue magic within the binding was the dwarves.

The Test of Fate

Fenrir made a quick decision to gauge the reaction of the gods, so he made a simple request. If the chain was just a joke, then no god would have a problem if one of them placed their arm in his mouth as he was bound. If the tethers broke, he would let the god go. If he sensed a betrayal of his trust, then Fenrir would devour the arm without a second thought.

The reactions of the gods only fueled the mistrust he had in them. No god wanted to lose an arm. The fear that crept in their eyes as he made his demands only cemented further to Fenrir that trickery was amiss.

Tyr was the only god who volunteered to place his arm in the mouth of the wolf. He trudged to Fenrir and gingerly placed his arm inside. The gods shackled him and waited for the inevitable.

The Removal of the Arm

Fenrir pulled against the chains, first to test out the strength of the bindings. They did not budge. This time, with his full might, he struggled against the chains, which only held him tighter. He could not break these chains enchanted with magic.

The wolf glanced around at the gods to see smug expressions of satisfaction on their faces. A part of him had hoped he was wrong, but he had learned from his father Loki to never truly trust an Asgardian. He looked down at his only friend, the one who had fed and spent the most time with him. Tyr looked miserable; the god did not share in the satisfaction that the binds would not break.

Burning with insurmountable rage from the Aesir gods and the betrayal of his only friend, Fenrir bit off the arm of the god of war. With a snarl, he swallowed it whole.

Tyr made no noise, but accepted his punishment with grace and dignity; after all, he felt his punishment for growing close and then betraying the creature was justified. He held his nub of an arm as the blood gushed from it, spewing in a pool on the ground. He moved away from the wolf.

Bound for Life Until Ragnarok

After the successful binding of the fearsome wolf, the gods moved him to a desolate, remote place where he would no longer be a threat. Odin led the gods to the land where Fenrir was to be bound until the events of Ragnarok. The entire way, Fenrir screamed and howled for his freedom.

The gods bound the massive wolf to a boulder. Fenrir continued to howl and snarl at the gods who had betrayed him. The last words before he could no longer speak were of violence and vengeance. He promised Odin that, when Ragnarok was upon them, he would seek out the god specifically and, in an act of vengeance, swore he would kill the Allfather with no remorse.

The words chilled Odin to the bone; he knew of the prophecy and how his death was foretold. The eyes of Fenrir burned with an unmatched hatred. Odin knew, at that moment, that Fenrir meant every single word.

Once the wolf had finished speaking, Odin drove a sword into his jaws to hold them open and prevent the wolf from talking again. The drool from his mouth created a river known as 'Expectation.' It was there that Fenrir remained until the beginning of Ragnarok.

Conclusion

The gods and mortals alike celebrated the victory of the gods of neutralizing the potential threat to Asgard. Tyr was especially celebrated for his selfless act, which further illustrated the character of the god. Tyr did not grow back his arm, but instead he kept the nub as a reminder of his duty and service to the realms.

The tale is also a cautionary one. Similar to Idun and her golden apples, it was important to be wary of those one may call a friend.

It can also be pointed out that perhaps if Fenrir was instead treated as an asset instead of a threat, things could have turned out differently for the pantheon as a whole. The tale served as a reminder as well that fate can always be changed if one dares to change it.

Chapter 9: Ragnarok

Ragnarok, also called 'the twilight of the gods,' is easily the most famous of all the myths in the Norse pantheon. The myth illustrates the death and rebirth of the gods. As terrifying as it might seem, change and death was the only thing that stayed permanent.

The Warning Signal

The Norns, Odin, and Frigg all knew the stint of Asgard would come to its end. The signals of the eventual downfall of the gods were prophesized, so they all were aware when the end of days was growing near.

Three Years of Harsh Winters

The first warning sign of impending doom was three exceptionally long, harsh winters in Midgard. Biting wind and snow covered the entirety of the realm for three years without reprieve. No spring, summer, or fall. The sons of the wolf Fenrir swallowed the sun and moon, resulting in a winter for both gods and mortals alike. The stars disappeared. The darkness had begun.

Starvation and disease plowed through the humans, and the desperation called them to do whatever they could to survive. Brothers slew brothers; fathers killed sons. The mortals entered an age of swords and axes. Violence erupted in Midgard, and that violence spilled into the realm of the gods.

In preparation for the coming battles, Odin asked Mimir one last time for counsel. There was nothing left to give; the fated time of the gods was coming to an end.

Death, Destruction, and Chaos

After the winter shrouded and darkness prevailed, the ground itself began to shake and tremble. The great tree Yggdrasil shuddered and groaned, as if ready to fall. The mountains leveled, and mighty trees were uprooted.

Loki and His Children Assembled

As the realms were covered in ice and snow, Loki and his children broke free from their bindings. Loki and Fenrir freed themselves from their bindings in the middle of the trembling of the earth. Jormungand, who had laid dormant for thousands of years, encircling Midgard in the depths of the oceans, rose from those depths. Due to the mountains crumbling and Jormungand rising to take vengeance, Midgard became an ocean wasteland filled with treacherous monsters.

Fenrir unhinged his jaw to devour everything in his path as he pelted across the land. From sky to earth, nothing was spared from his destruction. Jormungand spat venom into the sky; clouds of acid rain poisoned everything in their path. Plants withered, mortals starved or drowned, and the very air was venomous.

Ragnarok was in full swing, and nothing stood in its wake. Loki captained the ship known as Naglfar made from the finger and toenails of dead mortals. On its crew were giants, ready to breathe in the poisonous, chaotic air.

The Fight Begins

The trembling of the earth allowed both Fire and Frost Giants to emerge and join in Ragnarok. The Fire Giants from Muspelheim crossed the Bifrost into the realm of the gods. As they streamed across the rainbow bridge, the Bifrost disintegrated. As the Fire Giants broke through the gates,

Heimdall blew into his horn, signaling to the gods that the time for the gods to fight was here.

With Surtr as the leader of the Fire Giants, they charged the gods with all their might. The blade Surtr wielded was hotter and brighter than the sun. It laid waste to anything that stood in its way. Screams of terror and roars of battle pierced the heavens as each side met on the battlefield known as Vigrid, ready for the final showdown between gods and monsters.

Both sides were locked in battle. Monsters fought alongside monsters while the gods fought aside members of their own. The fallen soldiers of Valhalla, known as einherjar, were ready for action and prepared for this moment in time. All the heroes of the Norse myths stood their ground at Vigrid, both slaying the creatures of doom and falling to them.

The Fall of Odin

Odin and Fenrir faced off in the great battle. Fenrir gnashed his teeth with lips drawn back in a fearsome snarl. The mighty and wise Odin fended him off for as long as he could. Odin dealt several hefty blows to the massive wolf, but in the end, he swallowed the leader of the gods.

One of the sons of Odin named Vidar saw the fearsome wolf swallow his father. Eyes blazing, he avenged his father. He wore boots specifically fashioned for the battle, made out of the scrap leather human shoemakers had discarded. Vidar held open the jaws of the beast. As the beast struggled, he plunged his sword through Fenrir's throat.

The Fall of Tyr

The god of war Tyr faced off against another wolf by the name of Garmr. Garmr was a hellhound from the aptly named Hel. God and wolf were locked in an intense battle on the field of Vigrid. Eventually, the wolf killed the one-handed god of war. This was a victory for the monsters, and they fought harder with the morale from this kill.

The Fall of Heimdall and Loki

Heimdall and Loki battled after the Bifrost fell and the rainbow bridge collapsed. Because of their strained relationship and Heimdall's mistrust of the god of trickery, the two engaged in a long battle. They dueled each other, evenly matched, until both gods killed each other. The reign of the trickery god was over, but so was one of the most important gods of Asgard.

Freyr and Surtr

After the death of the beloved overseer of Asgard, Freyr battled against the Fire Giant leader Surtr. The god of fertility fought valiantly against his foe, but his strength and his sword were no match for the Fire Giant. After he killed Freyr, the skies glowed with a crimson red light in place of the previously dark skies. One more god had fallen.

The Fall of Thor and the Serpent

The last god to fall was Thor, which was the climax of Ragnarok. Eternal enemies Thor and Jormungand engaged in one final battle to the death. As Odin battled Fenrir and fell, his oldest son Thor fought against the serpent. Thor crushed his hammer Mjolnir into the skull of the serpent repeatedly while dodging the poisonous gasses and venom from Jormungand. After so many blows, the serpent lay dead in front of the god of thunder. Thor, badly beaten and his blood ladened with poison, staggered for nine steps before falling dead himself.

After the fall of Thor, the Fire Giant was felled. Before his inevitable passing, he hurled one last fireball at Midgard. The fireball scorched everything in its path on the remaining earth.

The New Realm

After Ragnarok and the heavy battling ended, the realms collapsed within themselves. The work from the initial creation was completely undone, and the only thing that remained was the abyss Ginnungagap. Or so it seemed.

The Survivors on the Plains of Ida

The surviving deities vowed to create a new and better world out of the little remains of the abyss that survived. Where Surtr had thrown his fireball and scorched everything in its path grew new lush, green vegetation. The Plains of Ida was the new realm and it teemed with life. Animals returned to the previous area of destruction.

Among the surviving deities were the sons of Odin and Thor: Vidar and Vali, the sons of the once-great Odin, and Modi and Magni, the sons of Thor. The beloved god Baldr and his brother Hodr emerged from Hel. After their resurgence, they put in the work to create the Plains of Ida.

The two remaining mortals were named Lif and Lifthrasir, who managed to escape from the hellish landscape of the battle between monsters and gods. Lif, the mortal male, and

Lifthrasir, the mortal female, repopulated the Plains of Ida and produced a new race of good, righteous men.

Conclusion

While the end of the world was dark and terrifying, the theme the Vikings wanted to hammer home was the theme of impermanence. Nothing remains the same; life's only promise is that it is consistently ebbing and flowing.

The Norse pantheon continues to inspire the lives of everyday humans. No matter the medium, be it video games, books, or films, the pantheon continues to dominate the fantasy genre. The introduction of gods and the creatures they encountered, for better or for worse, continues to inspire others to follow in the tradition of storytelling. Storytelling is an integral part of the human condition; it is a gift that continues to be in demand. From our ancestors to future generations, the ability to tell a good story, no matter the initial source, will continue until we meet our very own Ragnarok.

References

Britannica, T. Editors of Encyclopaedia (2021, July 8). Loki. Encyclopedia Britannica. https://www.britannica.com/topic/Loki

Christensen, C. (n.d.). This is Why Odin Sacrificed His Eye in Norse Mythology. *Scandinavia Facts*. Retrieved July 17, 2022, from https://scandinaviafacts.com/this-is-why-odin-sacrificed-his-eye/

Dan. (n.d.-a). The Binding of Fenrir. *Norse Mythology for Smart People*. Retrieved July 18, 2022, from https://norse-mythology.org/tales/the-binding-of-fenrir/

Dan. (n.d.-b). The Kidnapping of Idun. *Norse Mythology for Smart People*. Retrieved July 18, 2022, from https://norse-mythology.org/tales/the-kidnapping-of-idun/

Greenberg, M. (2020, November 30). *War Between the Aesir and Vanir Gods: The Complete Guide.* https://mythologysource.com/aesir-vanir-war/

Greenberg, M. (2021, February 16). *Vanir Gods and Goddesses: Read this Complete Guide (2022).* https://mythologysource.com/vanir-gods-and-goddesses/

Groenveld, E. (2017, November 2). *Norse Mythology*. World History Encyclopedia. https://www.worldhistory.org/Norse_Mythology/

Hanson, M. (2016, October 27). *Norse Mythology Facts and Information | English History*. https://englishhistory.net/vikings/norse-mythology/

Hirst, K. (2019, February 2). *The Myth of Ragnarok: Folk Memory of an Ecological Disaster?* ThoughtCo. https://www.thoughtco.com/ragnaroek-norse-myth-4150300

Liam. (2022, January 21). The Creation Myth of Norse Mythology (The Nine Realms). *Norse Mythology & Viking History*. https://vikingr.org/norse-cosmology/norse-creation-myth

Loki | Mythology, Powers, & Facts | BritannicaA. (n.d.). Retrieved July 11, 2022, from https://www.britannica.com/topic/Loki

Mark, J. J. (2018, December 20). *Nine Realms of Norse Cosmology*. World History Encyclopedia. https://www.worldhistory.org/article/1305/nine-realms-of-norse-cosmology/

Mark, J. J. (2021a, September 10). *Idunn*. World History Encyclopedia. https://www.worldhistory.org/Idunn/

Mark, J. J. (2021b, September 21). *Ten Norse Mythology Facts You Need to Know*. World History Encyclopedia. https://www.worldhistory.org/article/1836/ten-norse-mythology-facts-you-need-to-know/

McCoy, D. (n.d.-a). *Bragi—Norse Mythology for Smart People*. Retrieved July 9, 2022, from https://norse-mythology.org/gods-and-creatures/the-aesir-gods-and-goddesses/bragi/

McCoy, D. (n.d.-b). Daily Life in the Viking Age. *Norse Mythology for Smart People*. Retrieved July 9, 2022, from https://norse-mythology.org/daily-life-viking-age/

McCoy, D. (n.d.-c). *Norse Mythology for Smart People—The Ultimate Online Guide to Norse Mythology and Religion*. Norse Mythology for Smart People. Retrieved July 9, 2022, from https://norse-mythology.org/

McCoy, D. (n.d.-d). Tales. *Norse Mythology for Smart People*. Retrieved July 9, 2022, from https://norse-mythology.org/tales/

McCoy, D. (n.d.-e). The Aesir Gods and Goddesses. *Norse Mythology for Smart People*. Retrieved July 9, 2022, from https://norse-mythology.org/gods-and-creatures/the-aesir-gods-and-goddesses/

McCoy, D. (n.d.-f). The Aesir-Vanir War. *Norse Mythology for Smart People*. Retrieved July 9, 2022, from https://norse-mythology.org/tales/the-aesir-vanir-war/

McCoy, D. (n.d.-g). The Vanir Gods and Goddesses. *Norse Mythology for Smart People*. Retrieved July 9, 2022, from https://norse-mythology.org/gods-and-creatures/the-vanir-gods-and-goddesses/

McKay, A. (2018, July 19). *Creatures in Norse Mythology*. Life in Norway. https://www.lifeinnorway.net/creatures-in-norse-mythology/

Norman. (2009, February 14). *The Origins of the Norse Mythology*. The Norse Gods. https://thenorsegods.com/the-origins-of-the-norse-mythology/

Ragnarök | Scandinavian mythology | Britannica. (n.d.). Retrieved July 17, 2022, from https://www.britannica.com/event/Ragnarok

Scott, J. (2020, December 3). *A Beginner's Guide to Norse Mythology*. Life in Norway. https://www.lifeinnorway.net/norse-mythology/

Sutherland, A. (2016, January 2). *The Golden Apple Myth And Norse Goddess Idun*. Ancient Pages.

https://www.ancientpages.com/2016/01/02/the-golden-apple-myth-and-norse-goddess-idun/

Sutherland, A. (2018a, April 10). *War Between The Aesir And The Vanir Gods In Norse Mythology*. Ancient Pages. https://www.ancientpages.com/2018/04/10/war-between-the-aesir-and-the-vanir-gods-in-norse-mythology/

Sutherland, A. (2018b, May 6). *God Of The Gallows And How Odin Hanged Himself From Yggdrasil To Know Secrets Of Runes*. Ancient Pages. https://www.ancientpages.com/2018/05/07/god-of-the-gallows-and-how-odin-hanged-himself-from-yggdrasil-to-know-secrets-of-runes/

Sutherland, A. (2018c, June 30). *Norse Goddess Sif Who Lost Her Golden Hair Due To Loki's Evil Deed*. Ancient Pages. https://www.ancientpages.com/2018/06/30/norse-goddess-sif-who-lost-her-golden-hair-due-to-lokis-evil-deed/

The Binding Of Fenrir – Myths And Legends. (2020, July 5). https://mythsandlegend.com/binding-of-fenrir/

World History Edu. (2020, June 24). 10 Major Norse Gods and Goddesses in Norse Mythology. *World History Edu*. https://www.worldhistoryedu.com/10-major-norse-god-and-goddesses-in-norse-mythology/

World History Edu. (2021, July 8). Ragnarök in Norse
Mythology: Meaning, Summary, & Cause. *World History
Edu.* https://www.worldhistoryedu.com/ragnarok-norse-
mythology/

www.ingramcontent.com/pod-product-compliance
Lightning Source LLC
Chambersburg PA
CBHW051008140626
46546CB00016B/1303